Betsy Byars

WHO
WROTE
THAT?

Betsy Byars

Rita Cammarano

Chelsea House Publishers
Philadelphia

CHELSEA HOUSE PUBLISHERS

EDITOR IN CHIEF Sally Cheney
DIRECTOR OF PRODUCTION Kim Shinners
CREATIVE MANAGER Takeshi Takahashi
MANUFACTURING MANAGER Diann Grasse

STAFF FOR BETSY BYARS

ASSOCIATE EDITOR Benjamin Kim
PICTURE RESEARCH Jane Sanders, Jaimie Winkler
PRODUCTION ASSISTANT Jaimie Winkler
SERIES AND COVER DESIGNER Keith Trego
LAYOUT 21st Century Publishing and Communications, Inc.

http://www.chelseahouse.com

First Printing

1 3 5 7 9 8 6 4 2

Library of Congress Cataloging-in-Publication Data

Cammarano, Rita.
    Betsy Byars / by Rita Cammarano.
        p. cm. — (Who wrote that?)
Summary: Describes the personal life and successful writing career of the
Newbery Award–winning author, whose memorable characters include Bingo
Brown, Herculeah Jones, and the Golly sisters.
    ISBN 0-7910-6720-3
    1. Byars, Betsy Cromer—Juvenile literature. 2. Authors, American—
20th century—Biography—Juvenile literature. 3. Children's stories—
Authorship—Juvenile literature. [1. Byars, Betsy Cromer. 2. Authors,
American. 3. Women—Biography. 4. Authorship.] I. Title. II. Series.
PS3552.Y37 Z6 2002
813'.54—dc21
                                                    2001008337

Table of Contents

Betsy Byars reading aloud with five of her grandchildren. Although reading to her own children had inspired her to begin writing children's books, she continues to write children's books even now after her own kids are grown up and out of the house. Her books are still popular almost forty years after she published her first children's book.

1

Planes, People, and Pets

IMAGINE HAVING A pilot's license and living in a house with an airplane hangar in your basement. Whenever you feel like it, you can just taxi out and lift off. One year, you even take an exciting trip, soaring across the United States in your glider. During the summers, you travel around, flying in the glider or acting as crew. In the winters, when you're home, you write books and based on the great experiences you've had, and the interesting people you came across. For author Betsy Cromer Byars, it's no dream—it's her life.

Byars started out with a poor impression of the lives of

7

writers and did not intend to become one. She recalls in her memoir *The Moon and I*, "I didn't know any writers— I'd never even seen one—but their photographs looked funny, as if they'd been taken to a taxidermist and stuffed . . . I saw many dust jacket photographs and it seemed to me that no matter how hard authors tried— the men put pipes in their mouths, and the women held little dogs—nothing helped. Authors, even my favorites, looked nothing like the kind of person I wanted to become.

"This corpselike look, I figured, came from sitting alone all day, in a room typing, which couldn't be good for you."

In the end, Byars became a writer partially out of boredom. The Byars family had moved to Illinois so that her husband Ed could attend graduate school. Betsy stayed home with their two small daughters in an apartment complex. Most of her women neighbors either worked outside the home or were students and didn't have time to visit with Byars during the day.

Bored and lonely, Byars got an old manual typewriter and decided to try writing. Although she'd never written anything creative, writing had always come easily in school, and Byars always thought she could write if she tried. She started working on short, funny pieces and was thrilled when she sold one to *The Saturday Evening Post* for $75. After that, Byars thought writing was easy. Reality set in when she didn't sell another article for seven months. Soon, she was selling short pieces to magazines like *Family Circle, Look*, and *Women's Day*. Branching out to longer works, Byars decided to write mysteries for adults. Unfortunately, she couldn't find a publisher.

When daughters Laurie and Betsy Ann learned to read, Byars started making up stories for them. A bookmobile visited the apartments once a week and for the first time, she paid attention to children's books. Finding that some of them were not very well written, Byars started to write her stories down. Byars admitted, "I'm sure I would never have written my books if I had not had children. My kids not only read my books and gave me their very frank opinions, but they were also very communicative kids, always wanting to tell where they had been and who said what, and all of that was very helpful." Not only did her kids provide good material for later use in books, but they also helped her remember how it felt to be a child.

Another draw to writing for children was that it looked easy. The books were short and didn't have many characters or plot complications, so Byars thought they wouldn't be difficult to write. She soon found out differently, but actually enjoyed the challenge. It would eventually take seven years from the time Byars began writing to when her first book was published.

Byars' first books involved such characters as a dragon, a dancing camel, and a traveling cat. They did not do well. At the time, she didn't know that books could be written about real kids with real problems. When Byars discovered this writing style, known as "realistic fiction," it had an influence on her own writing. After that, her books were a success. Few children's authors in the 1960s and 1970s wrote about kids with absent or neglectful parents or children dealing with divorce. Not only was Byars good at handling difficult subjects, but she managed to do it with some humor.

Byars often gives characters funny quirks when they are dealing with a painful situation. In one book, a boy

Byars would get books for her daughters from a bookmobile, much like the one pictured here that would visit their apartment every week.

copes with his family problems by inventing cartoons. The main character in another makes up horror movies, while another one even imagines commercials broadcasting his embarrassments to the world. Another trait that makes Byars' characters unforgettable are the fun and unusual names she gives them—names like Cracker, Goat, Bingo, Figgy, Mouse, Herculeah, Meat, and Mud. But what ultimately makes Byars a popular author is her ability to make her characters interesting and realistic. A writer for the *New York Times Book Review* wrote, "Byars has the uncanny ability to know the secret lives, the outward postures, and the exact words her characters would surely use."

Maybe you've read about the adventures of Bingo Brown, the Blossom family or Herculeah Jones. You may also have seen one of the many television movies based on her books. If you have, then you've experienced parts of Betsy Byars' own life. She loves to put real events and people in her books. Some other real-life experiences she put in her books are her love of snakes, a dog being put on trial for murder, and the ninety-year-old twin sisters who still dress alike in *The Pinballs*. When Byars saw the real sisters, she was on a trip with her husband and had hurried into a grocery store. She remembers, "I came face-to-face with two elderly twins . . . they were dressed exactly alike—their hair was alike, their shoes and their purses. When I got back to the airport, Ed said as usual, 'Where have you been?' I said 'I have just been following the two most interesting people I have ever seen in my life, and as soon as I can, I'm going to put them in a book.'"

Many adults collect stamps or art or any number of different kinds of items. Betsy Cromer Byars collects interesting bits of information, and many of them end up in her books. Sometimes they are things she reads about or hears on the news. When Byars lived in West Virginia, there was a news report about a man people called the "Goat Man" who refused to let his house be destroyed to make room for a highway. The idea for her book *After the Goat Man* started with that story.

Besides the news, Byars gets her ideas "from the things that happen to me, to my kids, to my dogs and cats, to my friends' dogs and cats . . . " In *Tornado*, she related a story about a dog with a pet turtle in his mouth just as it happened to her own kids, and one daughter's attempt to drill through a school wall to her best friend's classroom ended up in *The Cybil War*. Including things that actually happened in real life is part of what makes Byars' books ring so true. In her autobiography, *The Moon and I*, she writes, "I often think of my books as scrapbooks of my life, because I put in them all the neat things that I see and read and hear." Some of the things she used were:

> "A man who could smell snakes . . .
> A woman who made varmint stew from dead things she
>   found on the road . . .
> An owl in the bathroom."

In order for her books to be realistic, Byars has to know what she's writing about. On her website, Byars tells aspiring writers, "When you write about what you know, you write with authority. The two words go together—author-authority, and what that means is that when you write with authority, you give your reader the feeling, 'This author knows what he, or she, is talking about.' That's very important."

Before she writes about something, Byars becomes an expert on the subject. Usually, her first step is to read everything she can find in that area. Even if it's some-thing she knows well, she'll read up so it's fresh in her mind first. If she's not very familiar with a subject, her next move is to go see or do whatever she wants to write about. She gets to go to a lot of fascinating places and events because she wants to use those experiences in a book. That's how she ended up doing things like going to rodeos or flying cross-country in a J-3 Piper Cub with only a twelve-gallon gas tank.

Did you know...

There are some things Byars wrote about that she didn't feel compelled to try first, which she listed in her autobiography as:

"Going over rapids in a homemade raft.
Getting bitten by a rattlesnake.
Breaking into city jail.
Flying off a roof with cloth wings.
Swimming in a neighbor's pool in my underwear.
Spending the night in a garbage dumpster.
Crossing the ice on a frozen river, falling through the thin ice, and drowning."

Looking back on her long and interesting career, Byars remarks that "it's now been almost forty years that I've been a writer, sitting in a room all by myself, typing. In those forty years, I've probably had every emotion there is. I've had moments of great satisfaction, deep disappointment, depression, elation, surprise, rejection, acceptance, fun, sorrow, laughter, tears—you name it, I've had it. I've had every emotion but one. In all those forty years, sitting in a room all by myself, typing, I've never once been bored."

*Throughout her life, Byars had a strong love for animals of all kinds.
Here she is at age 6 with a rabbit.*

2

Miss Harriet, Bubba, and the Zoo

BETSY WAS BORN to Nan and Guy Cromer on August 7, 1928, in Charlotte, North Carolina. On her website, Byars writes, "I was born in the same year as bubble gum and Mickey Mouse, 1928, a very good year for all three of us." Her first few years were spent exploring the neighborhood around 915 Magnolia Avenue, where the Cromer family lived in a bungalow. Betsy had an older sister, Nancy, who was two-and-a-half years old when Betsy was born. Their father planned for both sisters to become mathematicians.

As befits a writer, Byars' earliest memory is of a book. Her father read *The Three Bears* to her, but he kept changing the words. As he read the story, the baby bear wanted to know who had eaten his corn flakes and the mama bear asked who had been sleeping on her Simmons Beauty Rest mattress! She later used that memory in *Cracker Jackson*. Cracker's father reads the same story to him but substitutes low-fat yogurt for the porridge and Serta Perfect Sleeper for the bed.

Betsy loved books, and when she was five, she was taught how to read by her sister Nancy. Nancy didn't mean to teach Betsy to read, but Betsy picked it up when they played school. Their mother Nan did some acting in amateur plays and arranged for five-year-old Betsy to take classes in expression, where she memorized and recited poems. However, the daughter would not end up following in her mother's footsteps, for, according to Byars, "I had not inherited her dramatic charm, and I soon was diplomatically shifted to piano lessons."

When she was five, Betsy was visiting her father's parents in the country when she saw something she would never forget. She went with her grandfather Cromer to "pay his respects to Uncle Joe." They arrived at the house and found a homemade coffin in the living room. Betsy had never seen a dead person before. On top of that, her grandfather picked her up and "my leg kicked out, jarring the coffin, and Uncle Joe's mouth popped open. His mouth was stuffed with rags." After that, said Byars, " . . . for a long, long time I didn't want to die because I was afraid of having rags in my mouth." Byars used the horror of this experience in her writing when she had a character relate a similar anecdote about seeing a dead relative at the first funeral he ever attended in *The Pinballs*.

When Nancy was in the first grade, she would tell Betsy all about her day when she got home. Her teacher at Dilworth Elementary School in Charlotte was Miss Harriet. One of the fun ways Miss Harriet taught her students about math was to set up a pretend store. She used orange crates for display cases and had the children bring canned goods and other products to put on the shelves. The students used play money to buy and sell products and learn about getting and making change. Betsy couldn't wait to go to school and be in Miss Harriet's class.

In *The Moon and I*, Betsy Byars relates what happened on her first day of school, two years after first learning of Miss Harriet's wondrous classes from Nancy. Betsy found out that there were four first-grade teachers in all—and Betsy's name was not called for Miss Harriet's class. Betsy could not imagine being in anyone else's class, so she got in line with Miss Harriet's students anyway. When it was discovered that she wasn't in her assigned room, the principal got Nancy and looked for Betsy in the other classes. When they found her, Betsy was determined to stay put. As she relates the story, Betsy insisted, "'I want to be in Miss Harriet's room.' There was a silence. I corrected my original statement. 'I have to be in Miss Harriet's room.' The world stopped turning for a moment. It actually ground to a halt. Then, in this awesome silence, Miss Harriet said, 'Oh, Let her stay.' . . . And with an audible click the world started up again." Her stubbornness paid off, for one of the memorable things that Miss Harriet did was to introduce Betsy to her favorite book, *The Adventures of Mabel*, whose main character fascinated Betsy. "Mabel," Byars remembers, "was everything I wanted to be—pretty, adventuresome, a good horseback rider and she could communicate with animals."

Betsy's father brought scrap material home from the cotton mill and Byars learned to sew fast. "I was making my own clothes by the second grade, although I have a vague recollection of not being allowed to wear them out of the yard. Betsy showed the same enthusiasm in her sewing that many of her characters have for their own pastimes. "I sewed fast, without patterns and with great hope and determination, and that is approximately the same way I write."

Did you know...

When Betsy was seven, her family moved to the country in Hoskins, North Carolina. Her father, Guy, was an engineer by training, but jobs were hard to find during the Depression, so he took work doing the bookkeeping for a cotton mill. Betsy loved living in the country, and there she was able to revel in two other loves, animals and sewing.

Animals were an important part of Betsy's life as a child and she wrote that "one reason I wanted to become an adult was so that I could have as many pets as I wanted. My list was long. It started out:
"As many dogs as possible.
At least two horses—male and female—and all of their colts . . .
Pet snake, preferably nonpoisonous."
The Cromer family had rabbits and goats. One goat, named Buttsey, used to follow Betsy around and would push Betsy when she was in the hammock.

As a child, Betsy was intrigued by snakes, and when she was seven, she owned one "for about fifteen glorious minutes." Betsy had big plans to work in a zoo where she would wear a safari outfit and care for lion cubs and other abandoned baby animals. In preparation for this profession, Betsy and her best friend Wilma set up zoo exhibits in the yard. There were always more specimens in the bug exhibit than any other, but they were not a big crowd pleaser. Byars remembers, "Slugs had a certain 'yuck' appeal, as did leeches (which we got by wading in a forbidden creek and pulling them off our ankles.)" Butterflies and tadpoles were both popular exhibits, but the snails and box turtles were the biggest attractions. Zoo admission was free, but Wilma and Betsy took it seriously and kept overturning logs and stones to find new attractions.

One day they found some leathery eggs in the woodpile and took them home. Wilma stashed hers in a mayonnaise jar in her sock drawer where her sister found them and her mother flushed them down the toilet. Betsy had hidden hers in a mayonnaise jar too, but had kept them concealed behind some rollerskates in her closet. When the eggs began to hatch, "the jar was allowed a place of honor in the center of the kitchen table, and we all watched . . . " It was a snake!—specifically, a bull snake, according to Betsy's father. "I held it in my hand," remembered Byars. "It was like holding a strand of electrified brown spaghetti." Betsy's mother made her get rid of the snake right away, so she set it free in a field. Byars' dream of having a pet snake wouldn't be fulfilled until she found one on her porch around fifty years later. She named it Moon, and the pet was the inspiration for her autobiography *The Moon and I.*

Childhood dislikes show up in her books as well.

During the summers, Betsy and her family would visit her grandparents in Charleston, South Carolina. Betsy had a best friend there named Louisa, and Louisa's brother was a bully named Bubba. The girls tried to stay away from him, but one day he followed them to the Charleston Museum. Bubba cajoled Betsy into touching a mummy and then convinced her that her hand would become a mummy hand—and that if she touched anything else with that hand, it would become a mummy part, too. When she became a writer, Betsy named a few mean characters "Bubba" in her books and never realized the connection to her childhood bully until a reader mentioned that she had to know a real Bubba she didn't like.

The biggest bullies at home in Hoskins were the Fletcher brothers. The brother in Betsy's second-grade class was eleven years old. The other brother was thirteen and in Nancy's class in the fifth grade. Betsy remembers, "Everyone was afraid of them—the teachers, even the principal. I can't remember anything they actually did, but what they were capable of gave me nightmares." Betsy later modeled the bully in *The 18th Emergency* after the Fletcher brothers.

Although Betsy was a good student, her main interest was in having fun. "Adults were always saying to me, 'If only you would take your piano lessons seriously.' Or, 'If only you would take your math seriously—or your English.' Or whatever! Enjoying things was just more important to me than taking things seriously." This included finding pleasure even in hard times.

The Cromers lived in Hoskins for three years during the Depression. One of the highlights for Betsy was her sister's birthday party. Instead of buying gifts, people wrapped up something they had and bring it as a gift. Betsy recalls envying the strange assortment of presents

An ad for celluloid cuffs from 1880. Though they are not used as much today, many workers in the 1900s used these to protect their clothing.

her sister received one year. One of Betsy's favorite things that Nancy received on that birthday was a pair of celluloid cuffs, which office workers used to wear to keep the cuffs and lower sleeves of their blouses or shirts clean. Betsy loved to play with the cuffs, and according to her, "My sister could get me to do anything by letting me borrow the celluloid cuffs . . . I hope someday to find a place in one of my books for the celluloid cuffs." But the smallest and most intriguing gift turned out to be a dime wrapped in paper from a notebook, which turned up later as part of a school gift exchange in Byars' book *After the Goat Man*. After those three years, the family moved back to 915 Magnolia Avenue in Charlotte where Betsy lived until she went to college.

When Betsy turned fourteen, her father bought a boat, which he named the *Nan-a-Bet* after Nancy and Betsy. The first time the family took the boat out overnight, Betsy's mother stayed home. The trip along the South Carolina coast was uneventful, but early the next morning the water got rough. Since her father didn't have much experience, he frantically tried to sail back in increasingly bad water. The girls weren't worried at all and Betsy recalls that they "sat in the cabin, laughing and composing our obituaries." That sounds like just what one of her own characters would do in the same situation.

Central High School in Charlotte was where Betsy spent four years "trying to look like everyone else . . . We wore dirty saddle shoes, angora socks, pleated skirts, enormous sweaters . . . and pearls." A typical day at school was, according to Byars, "spent arranging to accidentally bump into some boy or other. I would rush out of science, tear up three flights of stairs, say a casual 'Hi' to a boy as he came out of English, and then tear back down three flights of stairs, rush into home ec and get marked tardy. I was tardy a lot."

Betsy also wore a lot of makeup in high school. During junior high, her father had talked her into not wearing makeup by giving her a twenty-five dollar war bond. She compensated for this lost time by piling the makeup on once she started high school. She and her friends pursued new beauty products with the same zeal she had previously shown for finding new zoo exhibits. During World War II, when Betsy was in high school, many products on the home front were rationed or simply not available. Stockings were impossible to find during the war because the material was needed by the military. One day, Betsy and a friend found their hands were stained from handling walnuts. They loved the brown color, and to mimic the look of stockings, they " . . . immediately started staining our legs." It wasn't until later when they tried to wash the stain off their hands that they realized it was permanent.

The only class Betsy remembers from high school is a math class where she was caught cheating. She had written the formulas on her desk. In addition to getting a score of 0 on the test, Betsy had to sit through an assembly about honesty, next to her teacher. She remembered that "I didn't mind the 0 at all, but the memory of sitting on the front row by the math teacher still makes me shudder."

In 1946, Betsy went to Furman College in Greenville, South Carolina to become a mathematician like her sister, just as her father had hoped. Everything went along fine until she hit a wall with calculus her sophomore year. Betsy finally got up the nerve to tell her father she was switching to major in English, but she still had no thoughts of becoming a writer. By her junior year, Betsy had transferred to Queens College, where she met Ed Byars. College rules were strict and she remembers that students "could only date on weekends, and even then, we had to sign out and say exactly where we were going and with whom, etc." Ed, who had graduated and was already

When Betsy met Ed Byars, she got both a husband and a love of flying. Here they rehearse for their wedding day.

teaching engineering, had an antique Stinson airplane, but there was a school regulation at Queens College that required written parental permission to fly. Betsy thought that this regulation was silly and decided to break the school's rule. After all, she wondered, "How could I tell a man of the world that I couldn't hop into his Stinson because I didn't have my mother's permission on file in the dean's office?"

Betsy married Ed three weeks after her college graduation in 1950 and "was very happy to be getting married instead of looking for a job. I had no work ambition." Even if she had wanted a job, Betsy didn't see where a love of reading and knowledge of old English words like *aungellyke* would help her find one. Throughout her childhood, book writing had sounded boring to her. The only kind of writer she had ever imagined herself becoming was "a foreign correspondent like Claudette Colbert in the movie *Arise My Love.* I would wear smashing hats, wisecrack with the guys, and have a byline known round the world."

Before Byars' writing career got off the ground, she and Ed lived in Clemson, South Carolina and would move frequently before finally ending up back in Clemson in 1980. Byars is pictured here with her daughters Laurie and Betsy Ann in 1953.

3

Books, a River, and a Fox

FOR THE FIRST five years of her marriage, Byars lived in Clemson, South Carolina and was a housewife while Ed taught engineering at Clemson University. At first they lived in metal, military surplus housing. Later, they moved to new faculty housing. After that, the couple built a home they designed themselves. Their two oldest daughters were born in Clemson—Laurie in 1951 and Betsy Ann in 1953. In the 1950s most American women spent their lives as wives and mothers and never pursued any kind of career. Women were told that their role was to help their husbands fulfill their dreams and ambitions, not to have any for themselves. Byars had no idea then that an exciting writing career was in her future. "I was extremely happy," remembers Byars of this particular time in her life. "My only writing consisted of letters and shopping lists."

Everything changed when the family moved to Illinois so Ed could get his Ph.D. "We rented our house, stored our furniture, loaned our dogs to Ed's mother, packed everything else in a red trailer and took off," recalls Byars of the move. "It was a little like going West and I was excited about it." Her excitement waned when she saw the barracks apartments where they were going to live. They were a big step backward from the home they had built in Clemson. Byars described the décor in a speech she gave in 1993. "The decorative highlight of the apartment was an ax on the wall with a sign saying, 'In case of fire, chop hole in wall and exit,'" she said. "I didn't want to wait for a fire, I wanted to exit then and there."

Byars eventually adjusted to the apartment, but she received another shock when she tried to make friends. Unlike in North Carolina, the wives in her apartment complex in Urbana, Illinois all either worked or were students. Like most American families in those days, the Byars only had one car. With Ed working long hours and the kids entertaining themselves with the neighborhood kids, Byars got lonely at the apartment. She remembers, "The highlight of my day was the arrival of the grocery truck after lunch."

Byars knew that she had to find something to do with her time. During difficult periods in her life, she had always done a lot of reading. This time, while reading the "Posts Scripts" page in the *Saturday Evening Post*, she thought, "This doesn't look that hard. I can do this." Byars got an old manual typewriter. The "i" key stuck and the "t"'s were too high, but that wasn't important. She set it up on the kitchen table. "I would push it aside when I ate and pull it back when I got through. I wrote constantly."

At first, Byars' writing efforts were directed toward popular magazines. She began by studying them to see what kind of work they published. Noticing that short, funny pieces were in demand, she wrote some and sent them off. The *Saturday Evening Post* bought the first piece she sent them for their "Post Scripts" page. They paid Byars $75. That was a lot of money in the late 1950s, and with it she "bought the oldest car in the state of Illinois." After that first, quick sale, Byars was convinced there was noting to writing. Reality set in when she didn't sell anything else for seven months.

This is an excerpt of one of Byars's "Post Script" pieces from the July 29, 1961 *Saturday Evening Post* entitled "The Sense of Humor":

> "Son, did you hear the one about the bunny who was going to have his tonsils out and he asked the doctor not to give him Novocain, and the doctor said, 'Why not?', and the bunny said, 'Becauthe I'm the ether bunny'?"
>
>   "No, I didn't hear it, dad. How does it go?"
>   "That's the joke."
>   "I don't get it."
>   "Well, you see the joke is ether."
>   "I don't think ether's so funny."
>   "No, but see, it's just a pun on the word Easter—see, ether and Easter and . . . "

"That wasn't great literature," admitted Byars of "The Sense of Humor", "but it does give you an idea of the two talents I started with: 1. An ease with words . . . 2. An ease

One of Byars' first pieces were published in the Saturday Evening Post *magazine.*

with dialogue . . . Everything else I acquired the hard way—I learned it." Byars was beginning to understand that she still had a way to go in terms of reaching her full writing potential. She said of her early writing career, "I was learning what most other writers have learned before me—that writing is a profession in which there is an apprenticeship period, oftentimes a very long one. In that, writing is like baseball or piano playing. You have got to practice if you want to be successful." Byars did practice— and ended up selling pieces to *Family Circle, Woman's Day, Look, Everywoman's Magazine* and *TV Guide.*

In Urbana, Byars and her daughters looked forward to the weekly bookmobile visit to the barracks apartments. Reading books with her daughters, who were then seven and five years old, Byars began to look at the books critically. Noticing that some of them didn't even seem to have a plot, she wondered how they had been published. Seeing poorly written children's books made her think she would have a good chance of doing better. That's how Byars started writing for children. She admits, "One of the reasons I started writing children's books was that I thought they would be so easy—they just seemed like nothing to me." This time, however, she didn't have instant success with her first tries. Rejections from publishers started piling up, but she wasn't discouraged. In fact, she said, "The harder I tried to write one, the more interested I became."

Byars told an interviewer for the *Contemporary Author Series* that she spent so much time writing while she lived in Illinois that "People who lived around us thought I was a professional typist . . . " Despite all the long hours spent on improving her writing, Byars felt she had to face the fact that she wasn't getting anywhere with her writing for children, and decided to branch out into other genres of writing. She was a big fan of mysteries and thought she should be able to write them well. She was soon disillusioned when Ed kept repeatedly guessing which character was responsible for the murder after reading only two pages.

Byars has written that during this difficult time that was full of rejections, " . . . out of necessity—I developed a

Ed, Betsy, Laurie, and Betsy Ann in front of the barracks where they lived in Urbana, Illinois. It was here where Byars started to take her writing seriously, enrolling in a writing class in order to try to concentrate on writing books.

kind of tough, I'll-show-them attitude that I have maintained to this day. Sort of—All right, you don't like that one, wait till you see this one. All right, you turned that down and you'll be sorry. I am now going to do the best book in the world." Despite her determination, rejection was difficult to fathom. Byars couldn't understand why no one would publish her books. "It seemed to me," she said, "that my manuscripts were a hundred times better than any children's books I saw . . . Probably, I thought, publishers of children's books only publish books of friends and relatives."

During her final year in Urbana, Byars assessed the state of her writing. On the plus side was the fact that her short articles were selling to national magazines regularly. On the minus side was the fact that she had gotten nowhere trying to sell a mystery or her children's books. It became clear that while her writing had come a long way, she still had a lot to learn before her books would be published. Byars decided she needed to shorten her learning curve by taking a class in writing at the university.

Byars looked forward to the class, but was hugely disappointed. She remembers, "I went to class on the first night with the greatest sense of hope and anticipation—not only because I was going to get some valuable professional help, but also because I was going to be in the midst of people who were writing too—living, breathing writers. The professor . . . started the class with this sentence: 'All the people in this town who are going to be professional writers are home right now, writing.' So much for my writing class."

1958 was a year full of changes for the Byars family. A son, Guy, was born that year, and Ed finally received his Ph.D. They also lost a much-loved dog. With Ed's education complete, the Byars clan was able to move back to their home in Clemson. A move had caused Byars to start writing, and a move back to Clemson may have made her stop. Byars was back home, with plenty of friends and activities. She no longer needed writing to occupy her time as she had in Urbana. Fortunately for her future readers, she still continued to write. "I had not been able to stop in Illinois, no matter how badly things went, because I needed writing to fill my life," Byars said of her writing before and after the move. "Now I didn't need it in that way anymore, but I still couldn't stop. Now the reason was because I loved what I was doing."

Byars' stay in South Carolina turned out to be brief. Early in 1960, the family moved to Morgantown, West Virginia when Ed was offered a position as head of the mechanical engineering department at West Virginia University. In taking the new position, Ed had doubled his salary. The Byars family lived in rented housing while building a home at 641 Vista Place. This move, like the one to Urbana, proved to be pivotal in Byars' writing career. Many of her books are set in West Virginia, and Byars credits her time living there with inspiring numerous ideas for plots and characters in books she says she never would have written otherwise.

Those books were yet to be written when the family moved to West Virginia, but Byars was about to write the manuscript for her first book that would be published. She wrote five stories about a dragon and sent them out to publishers. Eight different publishers rejected the stories. When she finally heard from the ninth publisher, a company called Houghton Mifflin, an editor there expressed interest. Even then, it wasn't an offer to publish. The editor only found four of the stories acceptable and let Byars know that seven were needed for a book. Byars wrote three new dragon stories that same day. Then the waiting began again. Finally, Byars wrote to the editor to inquire about her manuscript. The editor informed Byars that she was looking for an illustrator.

One cold, snowy morning several months later, Byars received her first book, *Clementine,* in the mail. "It was a moment of absolute magic . . . " remembers Byars of finally having her first published book in her hands. "It was completely, absolutely, unforgettable—magic. I was an author at last." All the hard work, disappointment and rejections were forgotten in that moment.

Unfortunately, she wasn't able to enjoy the feeling for long. A clipping service advertisement arrived in the mail the same day as her book. Clipping services used to send authors copies of articles in newspapers and magazines that mentioned their name or anything else they requested. Byars found the clipping service ad irresistible. It read, "We know what they're saying about your book. Don't you want to know, too?" Byars knew soon enough. The reviews of *Clementine* were poor. One scathing review included the line, " . . . only libraries with unlimited budgets should even consider buying *Clementine.*" Unfortunately, there are no libraries with unlimited budgets. Essentially, the review was telling libraries not to waste their money on acquiring Byars' book.

After reading the reviews, Byars came down to earth, realizing that her writing still needed a lot of work. In 1965, Viking published her second book, *The Dancing Camel,* and followed it with *Rama, the Gypsy Cat. The Groober* was published next, this time by Harper and Row. That was the first book Byars illustrated herself. Byars now had four books published and had found three different

Did you know...

A turning point came when Byars took a children's literature class and discovered realistic fiction. Until then, her stories had been about things like a cat's travels and a camel that danced. She hadn't known it was possible to write real books about real kids with real problems. The next book she wrote was *Trouble River*, a journey book. Byars liked the idea of writing a journey book, as she found them to be " . . . one of the easiest kinds of books to write. You start your characters out at point A, take them to point B, and let them have some adventures along the way." Byars knew she still had a lot to learn about writing well and that she didn't know how to go about maneuvering through a complicated plot. She soon received help from Annis Duff, a gifted editor. Byars was quick to make whatever changes Annis suggested. "If she said, 'Cut,' I cut. If she said, 'Add a character,' I added . . . If she said, 'I'm not sure this will be a publishable book,' as she did with *Trouble River*, I wept." *Trouble River* is about a boy left alone with his grandmother in a frontier cabin. When danger arrives, he takes her on a treacherous ride down the river to safety. Duff helped Byars make *Trouble River* into a book that could be published.

publishers to believe in her books. Unfortunately, none of them did well, although *Rama, the Gypsy Cat* had received some positive comments.

Up to that point, Byars had found it difficult to get the images she had in her head about a story to translate properly onto paper. Scenes that seemed funny or sad as she imagined them in her head often didn't seem to come out that way when she'd written them down. All that changed when she wrote *The Midnight Fox*. *The Midnight Fox* marked the first time Byars was able to transfer ideas from her mind onto paper. Byars recalls, "It gave me a confidence I had not had before. I knew now that I was going to be able to do some of the things I wanted to do, some of the things I had not had the courage and skill to try. For this reason, and others, it remains my favorite of my books." Another reason *The Midnight Fox* is her favorite is that, for the first time, she put a lot of herself and her children in a book. The story came from an experience Byars had in the woods in West Virginia when she had suddenly found herself face-to-face with a fox, which she found mesmerizing. The novel is about a boy who reluctantly stays on a farm with relatives while his parents bicycle through Europe for the summer. He's bored until he sees a black fox one day and ends up saving it. Byars wrote *The Midnight Fox* after *Trouble River*, but because of problems with *Trouble River*, *The Midnight Fox* was published first.

Both *The Midnight Fox* and *Trouble River* were successful books and were named Books of the Year by the Child Study Association of America. The American Library Association named *Trouble River* a Notable Book in 1969 as well.

Byars at the Newbery Award banquet. **The Summer of the Swans** *didn't take off immediately, but that all changed when Byars received word that the book had won the prestigious Newbery Medal. After receiving this recognition, she was able to pursue writing full time.*

4

Swan Time

IN 1968, THE year *The Midnight Fox* came out, Byars made another one of those changes in her life that unexpectedly moved her writing career forward. This time, she volunteered to tutor children with learning difficulties. The program was run by West Virginia University and was to change her life in ways she couldn't have possibly imagined when she signed up. Byars was assigned to a boy in the first grade and a girl in the third grade. Since school had always been easy for Byars, she was amazed to learn about the problems these children had. In the *Something About the Author*

Autobiography Series, she wrote, "This was a stunning experience for me. I had never been around kids who were having real problems in learning. I had not been aware of how much they suffered, not only because they had learning difficulties, but—more importantly— because of the way other kids treated them."

Byars' experiences with those kids moved her to write her most acclaimed book, *The Summer of the Swans*. The book is about a teenage girl, Sara, and her mentally challenged little brother Charlie. The children and their older sister live with their aunt. The action revolves around Charlie, who is mute, and what happens when he wanders off one night to find the swans he had seen with his sister.

Charlie is the center of the plot, but Sara's character is the one that changes. Byars crafted an intricate story in *The Summer of the Swans*. An excerpt from an early section of the book explains Sara's unhappy state:

> "Up until this year, it seemed, her life had flowed along
> with rhythmic evenness . . . She had loved her sister
> without envy, her aunt without finding her coarse, her
> brother without pity. Now all that was changed. She
> was filled with a discontent, an anger about herself, her
> life, her family, that made her think she would never be
> content again."

As the story unfolds, Sara takes Charlie to visit a group of swans that have landed on a nearby lake. Charlie is captivated by the swans and, thinking he knows the way back, he leaves home that night to find them again. He becomes lost and the rest of the book is about the search for Charlie and the changes in Sara that are brought about by the search.

By the time she got the idea for *The Summer of the Swans*, all of Byars' four children were in school and she did her writing during the school day. As usual when she had an idea for a book, Byars started out by doing her research. She began in the Medical Library of West Virginia University. "I found three case histories of kids who had had brain damage because of high-fevered illnesses when they were babies," Byars wrote about her research for *The Summer of the Swans*, "and that's where Charlie came from. All the details of his life were from those three case histories. I made nothing up." Many ideas from real life found their way into this tremendously successful book—the children she tutored, real case histories, and even the swans. Byars got the idea of the swans from an article in a Furman University alumni magazine. The piece was about swans that persisted in leaving the lovely lake at the university for other, less attractive area ponds. Furman University is in Greenville, South Carolina, but Byars set the story, like many of her books, in West Virginia.

Even the part about the search for Charlie came from another article, this one in a local newspaper in West Virginia. It involved an elderly man who left a picnic and became lost in the mountains. The search involved hundreds of people. The ending to the story was that the man was found at home in bed, and had never been lost at all. He'd just become bored at the picnic and left. Even though the story in the article ended in an anticlimactic way, the writer in Byars saw the potential in the idea.

Byars was proud of her work on *The Summer of the Swans*, but it was published in 1970, by her own account, " . . . to a sort of resounding thud. It didn't sell well, it didn't get great reviews; in some papers it didn't get reviewed at all." The poor reception *The Summer of the Swans* received caused Byars to become discouraged and wonder if she was on the right track. Even though she had had seven books published at that time, Byars was hardly living the popular image of a writer's life. She still didn't know any other writers and had never even met one of her editors, as all business with her publishers was handled by letter or telephone. After *Swans*, she even worried that she might never be a first-rate writer and considered another career. That's when she decided to obtain a master's degree in Special Education at West Virginia University.

Everything changed one morning early in 1971, as Byars was getting ready to go to a class. She recalls that " . . . the phone rang. I answered it, and a woman's voice said, 'This is Sara Fenwick and I'm Chairman of the Newbery-Caldecott Committee.'" She told Byars that she had won the coveted Newbery Medal for *The Summer of the Swans*. "I was stunned," said Byars of her immediate reaction. "I went blank. I couldn't say a word. She said, 'Mrs. Byars, are you there?' I managed to say, 'Yes.' She said, 'Mrs. Byars, have you ever heard of the Newbery Medal?' I said, 'Yes.' Obviously, it was not one of my shining hours."

No one was home when Byars got the incredible news that she had won a Newbery. "Still," she said as she related the experience in her Newbery acceptance speech, "you would be amazed at how pleased dogs and cats look when you turn to them and say, 'Listen, I just won the Newbery Medal.'" Ever practical, Byars wasn't even going to attend the champagne reception held in Los Angeles to announce the winner. (The actual award ceremony took place months later.) Byars' editor convinced her that she had to go to the

West Virginia University brought the Byars to Morgantown by offering Ed a teaching position, but it was the special education class that Betsy volunteered to tutor that helped inspire the characters in **The Summer of the Swans,** *as well as her research at the university's medical libraries.*

reception. Byars was very nervous when she got to L.A. The winner's name was kept secret, so she ended up staying hidden until the award was announced. Once the announcement took place, it changed Byars' life drastically. "Up until this time I had had a few letters from kids," she said in contrasting her life before and after winning the Newbery Medal. "Now . . . I got tapes, questionnaires, invitations to speak, invitations to visit schools, requests for interviews. For the first time in my life, I started feeling like an author."

Byars received the award that June in Dallas and was very nervous about having to give a speech. To help her with her nerves, writer and illustrator Don Freeman gave her a smooth, black stone he called a "calming stone," which she still has to this day. The large, elegant room was filled with 1800 people. Byars later recounted a funny story about the event, which began with two teenage boys carrying banners and wearing royal-looking

Did you know...

Byars is a master storyteller in her life as well as in fiction. The other item about the award ceremony that stands out in her mind is that they served her favorite dessert, blueberry cheesecake. She was too nervous to eat anything before her speech and felt like weeping when she saw the dessert because she knew she wouldn't be able to eat even one bite. Toward the end of her speech, Byars started to think about the cheesecake and how delicious it would be. Ed later told her she started reading her speech too quickly at the end, and she knew it was because she wanted to get to the cheesecake. As it was, she raced to her table, only to find the cheesecake gone!

pageboy costumes. They led a kind of pageant of the guests who would sit at the head table. One of the boys carried a banner with a gorgeous swan on it that was made of real, hand-sewn feathers. Byars was elated and felt like she was back in the Middle Ages until one of the kids harshly brought her back to the present by saying, "I could just kill my mom for making me do this."

In her speech, Byars related a humorous account of the stages she goes through when she writes a book. First, she said, " . . . I mainly sit around and stare at a spot on the wall or at my thumbnail." Of course she thinks about the book while she stares, but her children used to have trouble recognizing her staring as a work-related activity. They would ask her to do things for them and get annoyed when she wouldn't. Byars said, "I can protest for hours that . . . I am writing a book in my head, but they will not believe me. And the situation will end in bad feelings when one of the children says, 'You just don't want to wash these clothes!' And, of course, there is no denying that."

The second stage is when Byars actually starts writing, and once she starts, there's no stopping her. "People who have seen me in this stage would never ask, 'How do you find time to write?' because it is obvious there is no time for anything else."

During the third stage, her initial enthusiasm winds down and the rush of words streaming onto the pages start to slow down to a trickle and finally stop coming at all. This is the point that separates the women from the girls, and Byars overcomes it with discipline. She's worked out a method over the years and that is to threaten herself by thinking, "All right, today you are either going to have to write two pages or you are going to have to defrost the refrigerator." Often, doing tasks everyone avoids—like cleaning out closets—does sound like a better option, and she does those things instead of writing. Eventually, something will actually seem worse than writing, and she'll start getting words down on the paper again.

The final stage involves taking what she's written and revising it into something considerably better. Normally, that's when she has had her kids read her books. When her children were growing up, the family practice was for the kids to insert an arrow pointing downward wherever they lost interest in the story. Her children were always her harshest critics, and the arrows in the margins even showed up in her nightmares. "I open a magazine or a newspaper to read a review of one of my books," says Byars in describing one such nightmare, "and find that the review consists of a great blank space, no words at all, and in the center of the space is a small arrow—pointing down. The possibility is enough to make one tremble."

When Byars initially heard about her Newbery, she imagined kids all over America flocking to libraries to take out her books. That vision faded when a child wrote, "Dear Mrs. Byars, I'm dying to read your book that won the Newbery Medal, but our librarian has made a display of it and won't let anybody check it out." As usual, Betsy had a good sense of humor about this situation, saying, "It was something of a come-down, but since up until that time I had never even been a display, I really couldn't complain." One of the few people not impressed by Byars' Newbery Award was her then fourteen-year-old daughter. When Byars received a questionnaire from a class that asked her kid's opinion about their mother receiving the medal, her daughter shrugged and said, "Well, it's no big deal."

Winning the Newbery was a very big deal, and it was just the beginning. *The Summer of the Swans* was also named a Junior Literary Club book, a Notable Book by the American Library Association, and was a Horn Book Honor Book. Finally having achieved a high level of success, Byars dropped out of the Special Education master's program to become a full-fledged writer.

The "Morgantown Monster" which was frightening people turned out to be a sandhill crane, like the one pictured here. This newspaper story was one of the many that would inspire Byars' stories, and the crane provided the inspiration for The House of Wings.

5

Wings and Things

BYARS' GOAL DURING these years was to have one book published a year. In order to meet that goal, she sometimes wrote two or three books a year since not all of them were publishable. Her next book came out in 1971 and was her first picture book. *Go and Hush the Baby* is about a boy who uses his imagination to try to soothe his sibling. With *The House of Wings*, which was published in 1972, Byars went back to middle-grade realistic fiction. The inspiration for *The House of Wings* came from " . . . a story in the paper about a huge flying creature which had swooped down at a local farmer as he came from the barn. A follow-up story about a huge flying creature that had crashed into someone's TV antenna." The final story she read on the subject was about the enormous creature scaring some kids who were riding their bikes. The creature was dubbed the "Morgantown Monster"—but in the end, the monster was discovered to be an injured sandhill crane. Once again, Byars' local West Virginia newspaper provided an idea for one of her books.

The House of Wings is about a boy named Sammy who is left to live with a grandfather he doesn't know while his parents move to Detroit to try to start a new life. Grandpa has an owl in the bathroom and a pet parrot in the kitchen. Feeling abandoned, Sammy runs off and his grandfather follows. Only curiosity about what his grandfather found in the woods brings Sammy around. It turns out to be a crane with a hurt wing, and Sammy and his grandfather come together to care for it.

Byars started her research at the library, where the classes she had taken in library science served her well in teaching her how to do research. What Byars wanted to find out was not how cranes lived in the wilderness, but how one would survive in a house. As often happened, the research expanded Byars' story idea. She found lots of stories about people taking care of injured birds in *Audubon Magazine*. She was fascinated that the people all remembered exactly when and how they found the hurt birds and the moment when they later set them free. Byars also loved all the peculiar habits of the birds while they were living in houses. There was a crow that liked to watch himself in a mirror, an owl that hung out in a bathroom and devoured moths, and cranes that ate flies off of screens.

The relationships the people developed with the birds they nursed were very special and they all claimed they could pick their birds out from a flock. "By this time," wrote Byars on the development of her story ideas for *The House of Wings*, "I wanted to do the book about the injured crane, but I also wanted it to be about one of these gentle, patient men who love birds so much they set them free." Byars has a special relationship with animals and it shows in her books. She is adept at showing the friendship between humans and animals and using that closeness to help the humans in her books heal. A common message seems to be that when we care for animals, we come to care about each other and improve our lives.

The Winged Colt of Casa Mia had a similar storyline to *The House of Wings*. A boy is stranded in a remote place again, this time with his uncle. The boy is a voracious reader and a good student and has little in common with his uncle, a former stuntman who lives on a farm. A pony that grows wings brings the two together, separates them, and finally bonds them for life. The idea for the book's setting came to Byars when she visited Martha, Texas. The Byars were there for a glider event and she loved the place. To Byars, " . . . it seemed to me that if you wanted to have something happen that you didn't want the world to know about, this would be the perfect spot. It was that kind of remote place."

The next book Byars published in 1973 was *The 18th Emergency*. The main character, Mouse, is about to be beaten up by the class bully, Marv Hammerman. Mouse is terrified and tries to give himself courage by remembering his friend's list of things to do in different emergencies. All the emergencies are about things Mouse doesn't have to worry about—like being stuck in quicksand or getting attacked by a vampire—but knowing what to do in those situations makes him feel better anyway.

Garbage Dog shows up in *The 18th Emergency* and is the

dog who ends up with a pet turtle in his mouth like what happened to Byars' own kids one day. Byars borrowed the name from a dog that hung around the door to the school cafeteria to get scraps. The bully's name, Marv Hammerman, was made up, but it turned out there was a real living Marv Hammerman, who called Byars. The real Marv Hammerman turned out to be a teacher. Not knowing that the bully in *The 18th Emergency* shared his name, he started reading the book to his class. Byars remembered, "He said his class was delighted to find there were two terrible Marv Hammermans, and he took it very well."

Byars actually based the Marv Hammerman character in *The 18th Emergency* on the bullying Fletcher brothers from her grade school when she lived in South Carolina. While writing this book, Byars was able to get beyond her childhood fear of the Fletcher brothers and she started to understand them better. She realized how difficult it must have been for them to be kept back and be so much older and larger than the other students. Because of this new insight into the brothers, Byars had Mouse come to understand Marv at the end of the book as well.

After The Goat Man was the title of Byars' next book and was another story that was inspired by a news report. Like the real-life man the media had dubbed the "Goat Man," Byars' character was about an elderly man who refused to leave his home when the state was going to build a highway right through it. Byars rounded out the story by having the man's grandson, Figgy, live with him in a new house provided by the government. When Figgy learns his grandfather is holed up at the cabin with a rifle, he and his friends take their bikes to go see him. While riding their bikes to the cabin, Figgy is hurt in an accident,

Byars' editor at Viking Press mentioned to her that thoughts of her daughter's wedding—and thus, lace—may have inspired her to draw and write her book **The Lace Snail.**

which then prompts Figgy's grandfather give up on the cabin in order to take care of him.

The picture book titled *The Lace Snail* was born when Byars took a class in etching. As part of an assignment, she drew a snail and later added some lace. When she saw the finished plate, she thought, ". . . hm . . . if I had moved the lace up a little higher, it would look like the snail was leaving the trail of lace." The book grew from that thought as well as from another event in her life. Byars hadn't noticed the connection, but an editor mentioned that Byars was working on a daughter's wedding at the time, so lace was on her mind.

Byars not only wrote *The Lace Snail*, but also illustrated it. The first set of illustrations Byars drew for the book was ruined when the sprinkler system went off in her publisher's offices. Fortunately, Byars had enjoyed doing the illustrations so much that she was thrilled to get to draw them again. While picture books didn't turn out to be her best genre, she loved some aspects of writing picture books. Byars told interviewer Ilene Cooper, "It's just a wonderful feeling to see all these bright pictures and realize that, in a sense, your words created them."

1976 saw the release of *The TV Kid*. Once again, Byars' fiction imitated her life. The lake house in the book was the Byars lake house in West Virginia where they always feared snakes in the crawl space. The main character, Lennie, watches television to escape his loneliness. He also likes to row an old boat to a group of summer homes that are empty in the off-season, several of which he enters after finding their spare keys. Inside, he plays with the games he finds and imagines that he is one of the kids who summer there. One day he is almost caught playing in someone's house and, while hiding in the crawl space, is bitten by a poisonous snake. Like most of Byars' other books since *The Summer of the Swans*, this one came out to mixed reviews.

Things changed again with *The Pinballs*, published in 1977. Like *The Summer of the Swans*, Byars tackled a serious subject in this book—one rarely written about at the time. The story is about three unrelated kids in a foster home and how they form a family. *The Pinballs* was highly acclaimed by readers and critics alike. In Horn Book, Ethel Heims wrote, "The stark facts about three ill-matched, abused children living in a foster home could have made an almost unbearably bitter novel; but the economically told story, liberally spiced with humor, is something of a tour de force." *The Pinballs* received eighteen different awards including The Mark Twain Award, and Byars had another hit.

Byars created three realistic kids in this book. Carlie, the most outgoing of the three kids, is prickly and hard to understand at first. Afraid to be hurt yet again, she doesn't let other people get too close to her emotionally. Gradually though, she befriends little Thomas J., whose twin guardians are in the hospital, and Harvey, whose drunken father ran over his legs with his car. Despite being a sad story about the emotional and physical abuse of children, Byars managed to make *The Pinballs* sweet and funny at the same time as well.

The Cartoonist, like *The TV Kid*, is about a boy who escapes his family problems by living partially in an imaginary world. Alfie only goes as far as the attic, where he makes up and draws cartoons. When he hears that his brother may move home and into the attic, Alfie is devastated and locks himself in to protest.

> ## Did you know...
>
> One of the "scraps" of Byars' life that ended up in this book was the elderly twins who still dressed alike that she once saw in a grocery store. She made the ladies Thomas J.'s guardians and named them Thomas and Jefferson after their father's favorite president. The presence of the eighty-eight-year-old twins adds an interesting and odd twist to Thomas J.'s story.

Byars' next book was the intriguing *Goodbye Chicken Little*. Jimmie's Uncle Pete is a quirky character who always takes a dare. The last one ends in tragedy when Uncle Pete drowns while trying to cross a frozen river, egged on by his drinking buddies. In this book Byars introduced the idea of individuality, which crops up in other books from this point. Jimmie's family has several people who march to their own drummer and his mother celebrates Uncle Pete's fun-loving spirit with a party.

Some of Byars' best lines about life and family are in this book. In describing the way Jimmie's mother feels about the crazy, sometimes troublesome characters among her relations, Byars wrote in *Goodbye Chicken Little*: "His mother considered every member of her family unique, an individual who had never been on this earth before and never would be again. The family was like a great, tasty recipe, and the loss of any member made it less spicy, less enjoyable."

Byars had been steadily publishing books for eighteen years when the year 1980 brought major changes to her life. The biggest one was that the Byars family moved back to Clemson, South Carolina. They had been in West Virginia for twenty years. During that time, Byars had gotten many inspired ideas from the local news, as well as setting most of her books in West Virginia. Even the room where she wrote had been inspiring. In describing her room, Byars wrote, " . . . I wrote in a corner of our bedroom. I had a huge L-shaped desk in front of a big window where I could look out over the beautiful West Virginia hills."

West Virginia had been an important part of her writing life. Now Byars was going to a new life in a small town house in Clemson and there wasn't room for her big desk. The spot where she worked, with its L-shaped desk and her mountain view, had been an important part of her writing routine. She was afraid of leaving those things she'd been accustomed to behind, and remembers, " . . . I didn't think I would be able to write without them . . . I didn't tell anybody, but I was absolutely certain I had written my last book"

Fortunately for her readers, Byars' story had a happy ending. "Two weeks later, in my new town house," she said, "I wrote the opening chapter of *The Animal, the Vegetable and John D. Jones,* the first of my South Carolina books." Byars' writing had once again survived another move.

Byars was always finding inspiration for her books in everything around her. For The Night Swimmers, *she named her characters after country music legends, one of which was named Loretta after Loretta Lynn, pictured here.*

6

From Swimming to Soaring

THE NIGHT SWIMMERS was Byars' next big success. The story started out as a mystery about a girl and her two younger brothers who are left on their own a lot. They start taking swims in a stranger's pool after dark and one night they see something mysterious. Unfortunately, Byars' story idea stopped at that point after numerous attempts to figure out what they see, and she recalled that "Unfortunately, I could never think of anything mysterious for them to see. The kids were all but getting water-logged, they had been in the swimming pool in the first chapter for so long. I was worried."

Over the years, Byars developed strategies for when a story wouldn't come. "The first thing I do," she says, "is go to the library . . . pulling down book after book. I read the first sentence in every chapter. Nothing. I keep going. More books . . . Nothing. Finally, I will come to a chapter that starts with a sentence like 'The phone rang.' . . . That's it! The phone is going to ring and it's going to be so-and-so, and . . . Before long I'm back in front of my word processor typing away."

Another early problem in writing *The Night Swimmers* involved her character's names. She had a father named Shorty Anderson, and his kids were named Barbara, Henry and George. Byars couldn't think of a story until she saw a certain country singer on television and everything fell into place. She made Shorty a country singer and renamed the kids after country music legends—Loretta (after Loretta Lynn), Johnny (after Johnny Cash) and Roy (after Roy Rogers). After naming the characters, *The Night Swimmers* started to come together.

As often happened with Byars' books, something that occurred in her life supplied a different direction for the story. She was packing to move back to Clemson when she found a diary her daughter had written during the fifth grade. Byars wouldn't have invaded her daughter's privacy as a child, but since her daughter was an adult and a mother by then, she felt that it was all right to read it all those years later. Every page her daughter had written had something about hating her sister. That caused Byars to recall the fights she had as a child sharing a room with her own sister. Byars' mother divided the room with a chalk line to prevent the two from fighting each other. Remembering the strength of sibling hatred caused Byars to rethink the plot for *The Night Swimmers*. Instead of being a mystery, the story ended up being about brothers and a sister who come to hate each other.

The Night Swimmers was a dark story about kids who lost

their mother and whose father is so caught up in his singing career that he's hardly around. The kids do sneak swims in someone's pool, but there's no mystery and the youngest boy almost drowns one night. Byars won the American Book Award for *The Night Swimmers* and it was a *Boston Globe*-Horn Book Honor Book.

There are many aspects of writing that appeal to Byars, and something she loves to do is to write title pages. She has a drawer full of them, some written on her early typewriters. Some of those title pages are:

- THE ONE WAY CAVE
  by Betsy Byars.
- MISS PINKERTON AND THE ORANGUTANG
  by Betsy Byars.
- THE APRIL FOOLS
  by Betsy Byars.
- THE MERMAID MIX-UP
  by Betsy Byars.
- THE PINK ACE
  by Betsy Byars.

The Pink Ace was going to be about a pig that was a pilot, but Byars now has no idea what she was thinking of for most of her title pages. That same drawer also contains newspaper articles and pictures that sparked story ideas at some point. Even though she can't part with these items, she has no idea why she ever kept them when she looks through them. She writes, "It's as much a mystery as why I have kept a clipping about a man who ate thirty-nine watermelons or this photograph of two beagles in sombreros or this story about a woman who put her very old hamster into the freezer to give him a merciful death and the next morning found he had eaten through a box of French fries and was having a ball in a vegetable lasagna."

The Cybil War was Byars' next book and it was a fun book, like the ones she would later write about her character Bingo Brown. Fourth-graders Simon and Tony both fall for their female classmate Cybil, and Byars provides a light, amusing story about what happens to the three. Byars had originally written *The Cybil War* in the first person, from Simon's point of view. When she already had a contract for the book and was going over it one last time, she found she wasn't happy with it. Byars keeps working on a manuscript until she gets it right, even if that means revising it eighteen times. She finally decided to tell the story in the third person. Byars said that while it doesn't seem like a shift from the first-person to the third-person point of view would seem very involved, " . . . taking a book that is in the first person and changing it to third person is not simply a matter of changing all the "I"'s to "he"'s . . . . The things Simon tells, and the way he tells them, were not at all the way I, as narrator, would tell them. And I already had an advance for this book! I had already spent it! . . . When I was finally finished, the only thing about the book that remained the same was its title, my all time favorite—*The Cybil War.*"

To Byars, characters are the most important part of any story. When she's starting a new book though, the plot comes first, and she says that " . . . what I'm looking for . . . is something with possibilities—like kids swimming in someone's pool, like a character lost in the woods, like kids in a foster home." The plot for Byars' next book, *The Animal, The Vegetable and John D. Jones*, would be kids vacationing with their divorced father. On the way to the beach, they find out their father's girlfriend and her son are going to be there, too. Byars wrote this book on the kitchen table in South Carolina. She handled the intricate relationships between all of the characters like a master. Any kid with divorced parents will be able to relate to this book.

For her next novel, Byars moved her writing space upstairs with a gorgeous view of a lake. Just as wonderful was the purchase of a new typewriter that remembered what had been typed and was able to go back and erase when necessary. In a time before home computers, a typewriter with that ability must have seemed like a minor miracle. She couldn't even cut and paste a paragraph or even a sentence, but just being able to erase a few lines automatically must have been incredible. If you made a mistake on an ordinary typewriter, there was no real way to fix it; you just had to type the page over. The first book she wrote on the new machine was *The Two-Thousand-Pound Goldfish*, which was published in 1982. "This book was a particular pleasure to write," remembered Byars, "not just because of the typewriter, but because I loved horror movies so much as a child that everyone said they would ruin my brain."

Did you know...

Like many of her male main characters, the boy in *The Two-Thousand-Pound Goldfish* had an interesting habit that helped him deal with a difficult family situation—Warren made up horror movies in his head. An intriguing aspect of this book is that he had an unusual problem. He lived with his grandmother because his divorced parents were political activists who had become terrorists and were on the run from the law. Some writers shy away from introducing story lines that are very current and may later date the book. Byars, however, was never afraid to write about such topics.

While the new typewriter must have been wonderful, Byars had purchased her first word processor by the time she wrote *The Glory Girl*. This story was about a family of traveling gospel singers and the one daughter, Anna, who couldn't hold a tune.

1984's *The Computer Nut* was Byars' first collaborative novel. The book is about a girl who receives a computer message from an alien. Byars' son Guy did the illustrations in the form of computer graphics.

Byars' best novels during this period dealt with very serious subjects. In *Cracker Jackson*, Cracker figures out that his old babysitter, Alma, is being beaten by her husband and tries to rescue her. Again, critics recognized Byars' characteristic ability to deal with such grim subjects with humor as well.

Sometimes, while writing a book, Byars will see two different directions for the story to go. When that happens, she has to decide between the two ideas. That situation arose while she was working on *Cracker Jackson*. Alma's husband had attacked Alma and her baby, Nicole, and they ended up in the hospital. Nicole was in a coma and Byars had to decide if the baby would live. She knew the story would be stronger if Nicole died, but she didn't want her to die. Years of writing dilemmas had taught Byars that answers would come if she was patient.

One day at a writer's conference, Byars received her answer. She was with another author before the meeting began and they were speaking to some kids. Byars remembers, "I could hardly concentrate on my conversation because I was listening to hers. She was saying, 'I couldn't help it! I just couldn't help it!'" When the kids left, Byars asked the author what she had been protesting about. She answered that a baby in one of her books had died and the kids were upset about it. Byars remembers, "I thought to myself, Maybe *you* couldn't help it, but I think I can, and

Antique airplanes in flight. In 1984, Byars finally received her pilot's license, after having flown with Ed in his antique planes for many years.

when I got home, I went back to my word processor and in the very next chapter, Nicole opened her eyes."

In 1983, the year *The Glory Girl* came out, Byars had another milestone in her life. She took her first flying lesson on April Fool's Day. Ed had been a pilot when the two met and she had flown with him for years, but had never learned how to fly herself. She had a fear of flying herself, but was determined to overcome it. Having hung around pilots and flying for so long, Byars thought learning to fly would be easy—but she found out differently. "Like writing," said Byars, "it turned out to be harder. Months after I had learned to take off and fly around and navigate, I still couldn't land." She persevered though and obtained her pilot's license in December of 1984. Even with all her writing awards and accomplishments, Byars found getting her license extremely rewarding and wrote that " . . . I am as proud of that as of anything in my writing career."

Byars with granddaughter Amy at Amy's school in 1984. At this point in her writing career, Byars wrote four different series because she couldn't bear only writing one book with the characters she had created. The Golly Sisters, the Blossom Family, Bingo Brown and Herculeah Jones all had adventures spanning many books.

7

Golly Blossom Bingo

EVERYTHING CHANGES IN life, including those things we make firm decisions never to do. Betsy Cromer Byars ruled out writing a series from the start of her career. She decided early on that she would only write one book about each main character or set of characters. She thought she would give each book her all that way and not hold anything back. That approach worked for her for almost 25 years of writing books. Then it stopped working. So far, Byars has created four different series almost back to back. She is probably best-known now for her Blossom family series, but that wasn't the first one she tackled.

Every so often during her career, Byars took a break from writing middle grade novels for kids eight to twelve years old and wrote a picture book. *The Golly Sisters* books were her first attempt at a third category of children's writing. They are books for children just starting to read on their own and are part of the "I Can Read" books published by Harper. The Golly sisters series starts with *The Golly Sisters Go West*, in which the two hilarious adult sisters go on the road with a song-and-dance show. Set in the Old West, the sisters live and travel in a covered wagon. They wear wonderful, outlandish dresses and hats and are very unusual and fun in their outlooks on life.

What turned out to be the first Golly sister book was published in 1985. The first book in the Byars series about the Blossom family came out the next year. Titled *The Not-Just-Anybody Family*, this book brought Byars back to writing middle grade novels. The Blossoms are a unique, amusing family consisting of the mother, Vickie; her Pap, her father-in-law who used to have a trick rope act in the rodeo; and the kids, Maggie, Vern and Junior. The kids' father was in the rodeo, too, but he was a bull rider and died when he was thrown. That's pretty much the only dark spot in an otherwise happy family in this book. Byars created a memorable cast of characters, including Mud Blossom, Pap's dog, who has a "misery hole" behind the front steps for when he's upset or in disgrace. Another memorable, eccentric character is Mad Mary, an old school friend of Pap's who lives in a cave and makes stew out of road kill.

The Blossom family books tend to center around young Junior Blossom's inventions. In *The Not-Just-Anybody Family*, Junior makes wings to help him fly off the barn and ends up with two broken legs. That doesn't stop Maggie from helping Vern break into jail to visit Pap, who had a mishap with the cans he collects from dumpsters. Nor does it prevent her, with a little help from Ralphie, from breaking Junior out of the hospital and into the courthouse. All of the adults have unusual jobs in this book, including Ralphie's mom, who owns a balloon delivery business. The book is full of unique characters who have one hilarious adventure after another trying to straighten everything out.

This Blossom family book wasn't without its critics, but Byars' wonderful storytelling won them over in the end. In her *New York Times Book Review* piece, Susan Kenney didn't find the book to be the comedy of errors it was billed to be on the book jacket. Listing the things in the book that she didn't find to be light-hearted, she wrote, "A grandfather who goes after teenagers with a shotgun? Children left alone to fend for themselves . . . A mother so careless she doesn't realize that if she is not registered at a motel under her own name her children can't find her?" Despite having trouble seeing it as a comedy, Kenney gives Byars her due for her skillful interplay of plots and delicate, lighthearted approach. The review ends with her concluding that the book is "Funny-ha-ha maybe not; well worth reading, certainly yes." A *Times Literary Supplement* reviewer saw the book as "a tough, entertaining American urban romance, in the best tradition of children carrying more than adult responsibilities and almost magically winning the day."

After writing *The Not-Just-Anybody Family*, something happened to Byars that had never occurred before: she couldn't say goodbye to the wonderful characters she had created. The experience was like having a fantastic day with friends and not wanting it to end. "I found I had been captured by the family as surely as if they'd thrown a net over me," Byars wrote. The next book, *The Blossoms*

Meet the Vulture Lady, was published the same year as the first Blossom book, in 1986. In this book, Junior builds a coyote trap, hoping to catch a coyote for which there is a reward. Instead, he gets caught in the trap himself and is rescued by Mad Mary, who takes him to her cave below Vulture Roost. Mary started living in the woods when her wealthy father burned the house down around him by accident. Pap knew her from childhood, but she becomes Junior's special friend in this book. He loves her high cave with the rock ledge front porch, the boxes of books and her varmint stew. A reviewer for the *Library School Journal* wrote, "This is a lively, likable family, handled lightly but surely by an author known for her ability to write believable dialogue and present the desires of her characters with humor and understanding,"

Byars enjoyed writing about the Blossoms so much that she wrote four books about them in a row. *The Blossoms and the Green Phantom* was next. This time, Junior builds a flying saucer and the family and friends rally to help him finish and launch it. Pap gets stuck in a dumpster trying to rescue a puppy in there and the family gains a new member, the dog named Dump. Readers hooked on the Blossom family must have been thrilled to have books about them come out in quick succession.

A Blossom Promise was originally written with a significantly different ending. Byars hadn't wanted to write a fourth Blossom book because she was certain Pap would die in it and she didn't want the responsibility. Her editor at Delacorte talked her into writing it, tempting her with the idea that four Blossom books could be made into a nice boxed set. But Byars' worst fears were surpassed when Pap not only died, but Mud did as well. Byars felt awful about these two characters' deaths as she read the galleys. Over

Did you know...

A Blossom Promise was supposed to be the last in the series. Everything possible seems to go wrong in this novel, and it's the most serious one. While Maggie is at a rodeo performing with her mom for the first time, Vern and a friend take a dangerous raft ride down a swollen river. Pap has a mild heart attack trying to rescue them and even Maggie's success in the rodeo is ruined by finding out her mother has a boyfriend. In the end, things turn out all right as they usually do with the Blossoms.

the years, she had learned to act on her instincts, and they were telling her to change the book. Not only did she feel terrible about the deaths, but there was also the problem of her readers. They had heard another Blossom book was going to be published and were already writing to her. In a speech, Byars recalled the letters that read, "'We can't wait to see what happens to the Blossoms next.' And it was like, what happens next is everybody dies."

Byars decided to change the book on a Friday, which was a big problem, because the galleys were due back to her editor the following Monday. Byars wasn't able to get her editor on the phone, but plunged ahead anyway. She wrote for twelve hours that Friday, all of Saturday and most of Sunday, changing about half the book so that Pap and Mud could live.

The reworked book was a success. In the *Los Angeles*

Times Book Review, Kristiana Gregory wrote, "This is the final, bittersweet volume in the Blossom Family Quartet, bittersweet only because the cast is so memorably quirky that you hate to say goodbye."

Thinking that she was finally finished with the Blossoms, Byars ended up starting a new series with *The Burning Questions of Bingo Brown*. Viking published this series. The name "Bingo" came to Byars while she was working on a book about the Blossoms. She liked the name so much that she saved it for another major character. Byars' characters tend to form in her mind once she thinks of the right names. Shortly after the name "Bingo" popped into her head, she figured out the story of how he'd gotten his name, and then how Bingo felt about his name. Byars then started to write the first Bingo book, which was published in 1988.

Sixth-grader Bingo has a habit of pretending to sharpen his pencil in class while he's really reading other kid's journal entries. Bingo also has the habit of falling quickly in love in this book, but he finally falls hard for Melissa. He relishes talking to girls, which he think of as "mixed-sex conversations." In Twayne's *United States Author Series*, Malcolm Usrey praised Byars' characterization of Bingo, writing, "Byars has amassed all the joyous as well as the troubled doubts, fears, questions, concerns, confusions, and enthusiasms of an 11-year-old boy . . . "

Byars' next book, *Beans on the Roof*, wasn't a Bingo story, but one about the Bean family. The Beans, like the Blossoms, are an amusing family with a girl and two boys—though unlike the Blossoms, the Beans live in a city. *Beans on the Roof* follows a certain pattern in Byars' writing. Her books usually either have one or three main characters, though she prefers writing with three. That way, she can switch around and tell the

Byars at work. The word processors and computers allowed Byars and other writers to rewrite things much more quickly and easily than typewriters did, which came in handy for Byars when she rewrote all of **A Blossom Promise** *in just one weekend!*

story from different points of view. *Beans on the Roof* is also a typical Byars book in that the action occurs in a short span of time. Byars usually likes the story to unfold in 24 to 72 hours. The Bean book does stand out among the others written during this period of Byars' career, though—it is the only one that did not turn into a series.

In the following year, Byars made Bingo into a series

character with the 1989 publication of the second Bingo book, titled *Bingo Brown and the Language of Love*. In this one, Bingo continues his romance with Melissa while his nemesis, Billy "Rambo" Wentworth, continues to be a problem. Bingo has other problems when he learns that his mother is pregnant and he won't be an only child any longer. Reviewer Fannie Flagg said of Byars' writing, "She makes it look so easy and natural, you almost don't notice it . . . You may think you are reading nothing but a highly entertaining little book, but in fact all the while, Ms. Byars is cleverly weaving in serious themes like puberty, unwanted pregnancy, changing roles for men and women in society . . . " On another roll, Byars published *Bingo Brown, Gypsy Lover* in 1990. In the third book, Melissa moves away when her father loses his job, and Bingo stays in touch through letters and expensive long-distance phone calls. His little brother, Jamie, is also born in this novel.

After *Bingo Brown, Gypsy Lover*, Byars put Bingo aside for a while and went back to the Gollys with *Hooray for the Golly Sisters*. This book continues the adventures of the Golly sisters and their traveling show. It's a funny, silly book that emerging readers will enjoy. The main characters are adults in this series, but they are so childlike that kids will be able to relate. Especially humorous is how the sisters get jealous and play tricks on each other, each wanting to hog the stage during the shows while trying to outperform and out-dress the other one.

In a 1993 *Booklist* interview, Ilene Cooper asked Byars what made her return to certain characters. Byars answered, "Because they're enormous fun. The good part about any series is getting to know the people. You never have to think, 'What are they thinking?' 'What would they do now?' because it's just ingrained in you. You really know those people better than you know people you are actually living with."

Did you know...

Byars had thought she was finished with the Blossom family after the fourth novel about them, and it was even announced to the public that the last book in that well-loved series had been written. As it happened, Byars found that she couldn't let go of the Blossom family completely. She confessed that "I got to feeling lonely for the family, and it occurred to me that there was yet another story to tell. I remembered that when I was a child, I had a dog named Mac, and Mac was put on trial for murder—his victim was someone's pet chicken." That incident inspired Byars to have the Blossoms put Mud on trial when the hamster that Junior brings home from school for the weekend mysteriously disappears in *Wanted: . . . Mud Blossom*. This book won the coveted Edgar award, which is given for outstanding children's mysteries. "This time," Byars said of the Blossom series, "I guess it took me five books to tell all I knew about these characters and to do my absolute best by a family I came to care a great deal about. Of course, when I finished the fourth book, I said there wouldn't be any more, and I was wrong. So . . . "

The Byars at home, with one of their planes in the driveway. Their cross-country flight served as the inspiration for Byars' book Coast to Coast.

8

Reaching for the Moon

BY THE EARLY 1990s, Betsy Byars's writing career had taken many different directions. She'd written short, funny pieces for magazines, tried adult mysteries and written books about animals. In the next phase, she had branched out to realistic fiction, picture books and easy reader books. She had also written three distinctive, well-loved series. But Byars wasn't through trying new areas of writing yet, and in 1991, her memoir, titled *The Moon and I*, came out. Byars didn't write this autobiographical book for adults, like most writers do. Instead, she wrote it for her main readers—eight- to twelve-year-old kids.

Even though this was the story of her life and not fiction, Byars was still able to make it fun and interesting.

Byars hadn't planned to write a memoir, but she had started writing a biographical piece. It was about a black snake that had shown up on the porch of the cabin where she used to write in South Carolina. Byars was thrilled about her snake companion and named it Moon. She had wanted a pet snake ever since she had watched that first leathery egg hatch when she was seven years old. Like with everything thrilling that happened in her life, Byars wanted to write about Moon. The first thing she did, of course, was type up one of her title pages—this one reading "*The Moon and I*, by Betsy Byars." She had a title page and about three chapters, but she had a problem. She had already written about a snake in *The TV Kid*. A character in that story was bitten by a poisonous snake, and she couldn't think of what other kind of story to do about a snake.

A telephone call resolved the difficulty. Julian Messner, head of an imprint of publisher Simon & Schuster, called Byars and asked her to write a memoir. He gave her complete freedom to write it however she wanted, and that made her think about Moon. She sent the pages about what had happened so far with her and the snake to Messner. He loved them, so Byars wove the stories of her life around her adventures with Moon. The reader comes to know a lot about Betsy Cromer Byars by hearing about her relationship with the snake. First, we find out that even in her early 60's she could still be as excited and curious as a seven-year-old about a wild animal. This is an endearing trait and readers will understand that part of how Byars writes for kids so well is that she shares their sense of wonder and enthusiasm.

The Moon and I also tells us other things about Byars. She doesn't try to put Moon in a cage or otherwise make a pet out of him. He's her pet snake only in that he's her favorite snake, as she explained to her grandson. She respects Moon and wants to get to know him. She looks for him, she follows him, and she watches him. She's excited when he appears and disappointed when he doesn't. She thinks about him all the time. Byars did manage to touch Moon, but was bitten for her trouble. Byars remembers that "I reached out and touched the tail. It was cool, dry, and smooth. The snake's skin crawled a little as if with revulsion at being touched. I encircled the tail with my hand . . . With the speed of lightening, the snake's head darted up . . . and caught my little finger. It was a move so stunning, so silent, that I felt no pain, just the sharp stab of panic."

After that experience, Byars gained more respect for Moon. Still, as a writer, she was dying to know what Moon felt like and wanted to pick him up. She had been too shocked to notice much when she touched him the first time. Byars talked herself into trying again the same way she talked herself into going on Space Mountain at Disneyland and doing other things she wouldn't normally do. She told herself she had to hold Moon if she was going to write about him. The next time, Ed held Moon's head down with a stick while Byars picked up Moon's thrashing tail. This experience was almost as bad as the first time except that she wasn't bitten. Moon wrapped around her arm, letting her know in no uncertain terms that he was very upset. Byars decided to stick to just watching Moon after that.

Critic Diane Roback, writing in *Publisher's Weekly*, praised *The Moon and I* as "an appealingly idiosyncratic narrative that seamlessly weaves together the Newbery winner's life and art." In the *School Library Journal*, Phyllis

Graves gave a glowing review as well, calling it "very special nonfiction that truly entertains as it informs."

The year Byars' memoir came out, *Bingo Brown's Guide to Romance* was published as well. Continuing the story of Bingo's romance with Melissa, this book is about what happens when Melissa comes back to town on a visit. The course of true love has a bump in that Melissa is mad that Bingo sent her a photocopy of a love letter. Readers enjoyed Bingo's continuing adventures, but not all critics shared their enthusiasm. One wrote, "More episodic than cohesive, this is nevertheless keen-eyed and better written than most series titles."

Byars' next book, *Coast to Coast*, took an unusually long time to be accepted for publication. Byars had wanted to write a novel about flying from the time she began writing. Flying had almost always been part of her life. When she was little, her father liked to take her to the airport to watch the planes taking off. When she met Ed, who owned a plane, flying, or at least soaring, was part of their courtship and became part of her life. Betsy and Ed spent many summers soaring. They traveled around and Ed soared while Betsy acted as crew chief. "This means," explained Ed of Betsy's role, "helping assemble by lifting wings and holding a fifty-pound wing tip over her head for long periods; polishing the wings; taping the joints; driving the car with a thirty-foot-trailer attached, while working the radio . . . ." One of the most difficult parts of the crew chief job could be finding Ed at the end of the day. Gliding is not as precise as flying planes with motors, and that is especially true about landing. Ed often ended up in a remote field and Betsy had to figure out where he was in order to get to him.

Did you know...

Shortly after Byars got her pilot's license in December of 1984, she got her own plane. Since Byars had a deep love of flying, she naturally wanted to write about it. She also knew a lot about the subject and didn't want to waste all that good potential material. Where she ran into a problem was coming up with the plot. She explained, "The only plot I could think of was something going wrong with the engine, the plane crashing and the people having to survive." There was nothing wrong with that particular plot idea except that Byars wanted her readers to love flying, not fear it. It took her a while to think of a better storyline, and in the meantime she put the project on the back burner.

One of Ed's other hobbies is collecting and restoring antique airplanes. That hobby materialized in the plot that Byars finally conceived for her book on flying. The book that would become *Coast to Coast* would be about a cross-country journey in an antique plane. The main characters would be a girl and her grouchy grandfather. Once Byars knew what the story was going to be about, she knew that everything else would come while she worked on the book.

Since Byars knew so much about antique planes and flying, she didn't need to do her usual research. Only one important detail was missing before she could start. She needed to know what route her characters would take on their trip. She asked Ed to map one out that night and recalled that "Within five minutes, Ed had air maps spread out all over the floor. It turns out he'd been wanting to barnstorm across the country like this for a long time." Betsy didn't share his interest in actually taking the trip across the United States, but Ed knew just what to say to get her to go. He told her she needed to go in order to be able to write about it.

They took the trip in a 1940 J-3 Piper Cub that Ed owned, the exact same plane thirteen-year-old Birch and her grandfather use in *Coast to Coast*. The little plane had two seats and Betsy sat in the one in front. Harvey, their dog, rode on the luggage rack. In explaining why they brought their dog along, Byars said, "We had our choice of taking luggage or our dog . . . We opted for the dog. We both knew there would be times when we wouldn't be speaking to each other and we'd need the dog to talk to."

The journey to California took seven days and Byars filled an entire journal with details for the book. The novel was going to be a journey book like *Trouble River*. This particular book, however, did not turn out as she expected. People might think that a hugely successful author like Betsy Byars could easily get anything she wrote published. After she won the Newbery award, Ed jokingly told her that " . . . she would never have to look another rejection slip in the face and could even get her PTA minutes published . . . " Byars would still occasionally get rejection letters after that, but said they didn't sting nearly as much as before she had so many books published.

Still, she may not have been prepared for the length of time it took to have *Coast to Coast* accepted. Byars started writing *Coast to Coast* in 1987. She said that " . . . after I finally, finally finished the manuscript and sent it to my publisher, they didn't like it. They said it didn't have enough

The Byars made their cross-country flight in a Piper Cub airplane, such as the one shown here.

plot construction." When she was writing *The Moon and I* in 1990, Byars had already rewritten the story about the cross-country plane ride approximately 17 times. Byars went through several plots and editors while she reworked the book, but she intended to keep working on it until it came out right. In the end, she was told to write a new first chapter and to get rid of the last two chapters—an idea she didn't like at all. She remembered, "I ranted and raved, and then I finally put a new chapter in front and took two off the back. And it worked, because if you start with a new first chapter, it frames the story." Byars' determination finally paid off and *Coast to Coast* was published in 1992, a year after her memoir was published.

In 1994, Byars' first book in a new series came out. The book was called *The Dark Stairs* and introduced her girl sleuth, Herculeah Jones. Herculeah is named after Hercules. Her parents are divorced and she lives with her private investigator mother. Her father is a police detective, and her sidekick is the loyal, overweight kid across the street, nicknamed Meat. Byars finally had a bona fide mystery published, 30 years after she first tried writing one. The Herculeah mysteries are light-hearted, with Herculeah's hair "frizzling" when she's in danger. She loves to shop in second hand stores and even picks up some old, thick "granny" glasses so she can "fog out" and think more clearly.

Something remarkable about the Herculeah Jones series is that the main character is a girl. Byars has written other books with a girl as the main character, but none of them were as memorable as her boy characters. Critics often remarked on the fact that Byars' boy characters were more three dimensional and interesting than her girl characters. With Herculeah, Byars created a realistic, intriguing, three-dimensional girl character. In doing so, Byars continued to grow as a writer, expanding in new directions. Another notable detail about this series is that Herculeah and her mother live in a neighborhood near the center of town. The setting frees Herculeah to be able to easily walk to stores and provides added interest and opportunities for sleuthing. Many of the people who live in her neighborhood have businesses in their homes like her mother and a fortuneteller down the block, for instance. But like many of Byars' main characters, Herculeah is solidly middle- to lower middle-class. Byars seems to have no interest in writing about wealthy or even upper middle-class kids. Her interests and sympathies are with families who, like most Americans, can't buy everything they want and don't live in big homes.

After the first Herculeah book, Byars published another emerging reader book about the Golly sisters and their zany adventures with their traveling act called *The Golly Sisters Ride Again*. Byars went back to Herculeah Jones in her next book, *Tarot Says Beware*. This one involves Herculeah's fortune-telling neighbor and her bird, Tarot. In 1996, Byars came started another "I Can Read" series with *My Brother Ant*. That same year, she published her third mystery in the Herculeah Jones series, *The Dead Letter*. The middle grade novel, *Tornado,* came out that year as well.

1997 brought the second Ant book, *Ant Plays Bear*, and the fourth Herculeah book, *Death's Door*, followed by Herculeah mystery *Disappearing Acts* in 1998.

Byars had previously worked on a book with her son, Guy, who provided the graphics. Byars had even provided illustrations for two of her books herself. Two things she hadn't done were collaborating in the writing of a book and working on a book with any of her daughters. All that changed in 2000 with the publication of *My Dog, My Hero*, which was written by Byars and her two eldest daughters, Laurie Myers and Betsy Duffey. Both Duffy and Myers were already established authors of children's books. So now Byars has worked with her children, who first inspired her to write, but considers working on one with her husband out of the question. She's convinced that it would be the end of her writing career and her marriage!

Betsy with her husband Ed on their 40th wedding anniversary. Byars credits her husband with being her greatest champion.

9

A Well That Never Goes Dry

BETSY CROMER BYARS has had a long, exciting, and successful career as a writer. Much of it does involve sitting alone in a room typing—just as she concluded long ago at how writers lived—but her imagination is good company. Some writers share their ideas and manuscripts with friends or family as they go along, but writing is a solitary process for Byars. From the time she gets an idea for a book until the time she submits it for publication, she doesn't like to talk about it. When her children were growing up, she used to get them to read manuscripts in their final stages and put that

87

small arrow in sections where they got bored, but that was the rare exception. She wouldn't even talk about them to Ed and he learned not to ask or comment. He wrote, "On occasion I have peeped at a manuscript left carelessly lying about and usually have thought it great and would have liked to say so, but did not dare." Even though she doesn't share her writing with her husband until it's finished, Byars credits him with being her greatest champion. "He always believed I would eventually be successful," wrote Byars, "and in the periods when I got discouraged and went back to school to get a masters degree, or whatever, he would say, 'Just don't close the door on your writing.'"

Byars' children provided a great deal of inspiration when they were growing up, but also kept her feet firmly on the ground. When her son Guy was almost eight, he had trouble sleeping one night. Byars was trying to work and Guy kept interrupting. "Finally," remembers Byars, "in desperation he said, 'You know, maybe it would help me get to sleep if I read some of your failures.' I asked after a moment if there was any particular failure that would induce sleep better than the others, and he named one . . . He read for about three minutes . . . and fell fast asleep. It was a humbling moment."

Early in her writing career, Byars used to wait for ideas to come to her. Usually, they came from something she heard or read or something that happened to family or friends. Occasionally, the wait for an idea for her next book was a long one and she would get impatient. "Sometimes," Byars remembers, "this waiting would go on for months. I would sit around, marking time, waiting like a tick for a dog to come by." The next phase was desperation, but an idea usually arrived just when it seemed hopeless. Once she had the idea, her imagination would be off and running. Later, she realized that it wasn't necessary to have a perfectly-formed idea or every detail nailed down in order to write.

The thing Byars loves most about being a writer is that she gets to be her own boss. In her memoir, she wrote, "I work when I want to. If I don't feel like writing, I can go swimming or flying or jogging to Mexico. I can go on vacation when I want, and if I decide to take a month off, or a summer off, or a year off, I can do that, too." But the thing Byars likes the least about being a writer is also the fact that she's her own boss. She doesn't think that she's

Did you know...

When she becomes stuck early in a book or is unsure how to start the next chapter, she looks through library books until she is inspired. Another strategy that Byars employs involves reading the manuscript as if she is an ordinary reader and didn't write the story. As she reads, she tries to figure out what the reader would expect to happen in the story. "For example," explains Byars of this method, "I may have spent two hundred words describing a tree just because I felt like describing a tree. But what I was saying to the reader was watch out for this tree! . . . I wouldn't have you read two hundred words about a tree if that tree wasn't going to fall on somebody or somebody wasn't going to fall out of it."

a very good boss, and has to resort to tricks to get herself to sit down and write—such as saying to herself "I say, Betsy, there's a writer in Kansas who is working on the exact same book that you are working on. A snake appeared on *her* front porch, and she also named it Moon, and this writer is not sitting on the sofa watching Road Runner cartoons like you're doing." She goes on to present herself with the horrible idea that if she doesn't start working immediately, she will one day be faced with a newspaper headline that the other writer won a big award for her book!

Byars has another ploy to get herself working when she has to make revisions. She says to herself, "Betsy, this Friday you're going on a trip, and when you come back from your trip, this same lousy manuscript is going to be sitting right there. And you know how you hate to come home to a lousy manuscript. Give yourself a break. Just rewrite the first chapter."

Something else that's great about being an author is that Byars receives some funny letters from kids. One of her favorites reads, "Dear Betsy Byars, All of us have to write to a real live author. Please write and tell me you're alive, or I will have to write a poem." Another child wrote, "I just have one question and it's personal. Are you human?" Occasionally, a fan writes to complain. One such letter read "Our teacher wants us to do criticisms of the books we read. And here is my criticism. Your sentences are clogged."

Not all the letters Byars receives are funny or critical. Since some of Byars' books deal with very serious subjects like abandoned or abused kids, she receives some more serious and personal letters from children as well. Of these kinds of letters, Byars notes that " . . . sometimes it's very

Byars speaking in Newcastle, England. Her storytelling ability extends to her public speaking, which makes her popular at conferences.

difficult to write back because you realize the parents might read it, and you cannot reveal anything that this child has said that might upset the parents."

No one can write 24 hours a day, and Byars has an active life outside of writing. Her hobbies include reading, traveling, and doing needlepoint and word puzzles. She and Ed especially enjoy going to Europe. They fly there on commercial airlines since gliders aren't made to cross oceans. As readers might imagine from her easygoing style, Byars is a casual person who likes to eat popcorn and dress in jeans and t-shirts.

Byars sometimes speaks at conferences for writers where audiences enjoy her humor. At one national conference, her audience was laughing so much and so loudly that author Judy Blume poked her head in to see who was speaking next to her and cracking everyone up. The same conference found Byars on the floor playing jacks with Blume and Paula Danziger.

Did you know...

Another helpful tip is to figure out your writing strengths and use them. Since Byars is very good at writing realistic-sounding dialogue, there are many conversations in her books. She doesn't include much in the way of descriptions of people and places because she thinks descriptions are one of her weaker points as a writer. Byars' habit of not providing descriptions of her characters can make things difficult for the illustrator, but only one has called to ask for descriptive details. Like most writers, she has limited or no contact at all with the people who illustrate her books. She turns in her manuscripts and the illustrators then begin to work. Even though Byars doesn't work with the illustrators and has had many different ones, she says that " . . . every illustrator almost without exception has caught the people perfectly. When I saw the jacket of *The Pinballs*, there were the characters. That was a stunning moment for me."

Byars shares her love of writing with kids on a section of her website devoted to writing tips. Her first tip is to read, and—just as her teacher had instructed her—to write about things you know. Once you've written something, she suggests reading it aloud to hear how it sounds. Byars notes that this is especially useful to make dialogue sound natural. When Byars started writing, her children asked who she was talking to when she was in another room reading her writing out loud. Another good suggestion she has is to pretend your story is going to be a movie and pick Hollywood stars to play the parts. If you imagine them saying the words you wrote, then you can tell if the dialogue sounds natural.

Byars has seen the children's publishing world change a great deal over the years. When she began writing for kids, books had to be wholesome and not very true to life. An editor even sent her a note telling her not to have a character tell a lie. Many serious topics were considered inappropriate for books for children, too. Today, Byars says, "You don't feel any pressure, you don't find yourself thinking things like, 'I can't say this' or 'This will be too tough a subject for kids.'"

Summing up the longevity of her career, Byars wrote, "I used to think . . . that writers were like wells, and sooner or later we'd use up what had happened to us and our children and our friends and our dogs and cats, and there wouldn't be anything left. We'd go dry and have to quit. I imagine we would if it weren't for that elusive quality—creativity. I can't define it, but I have found from experience that the more you use it, the better it works."

1928 Betsy Alice Cromer born August 7 in Charlotte, North Carolina

1935 Cromer family moves to Hoskins Mill

1938 Cromer family moves back to Charlotte

1946 Graduates from Central High School
Attends Furman University in Greenville, South Carolina

1947 Transfers to Queens College in Charlotte

1949 Meets Ed Byers

1950 Graduates with B.A. in English
Marries Ed Byars
Moves to Clemson, South Carolina

1951 First child, daughter Nancy Laura (Laurie) is born

1952 Daughter Betsy Ann is born

1956 Byars family moves to Urbanna, Illinois
Daughter Nan Aline is born
Starts writing articles

1958 Son Guy Ford is born
Byars family moves back to Clemson
Has piece published in the *Saturday Evening Post*

1960 Family moves to Morgantown, West Virginia

1962 *Clementine*

1965 *The Dancing Camel*

1966 *Rama, The Gypsy Cat*

1967 *The Groober*

1968 *The Midnight Fox*

1969 *Trouble River*

1970 *The Summer of the Swans*

1971 Receives the Newbery Medal for *Summer of the Swans*
Go and Hush the Baby
Writes and directs an Operetta for her mentally challenged students

1972 *House of Wings*

1973 *The 18th Emergency*
The Winged Colt of Casa Mia

1974 *After the Goat Man*

1975 *The Lace Snail*

1976 *The TV kid*

1977 *The Pinballs*

1978 *The Cartoonist*

1979 *Goodbye, Chicken Little*

1980 Family moves to Clemson
The Night Swimmers

1981 Receives the American Book Award for *The Night Swimmers*
The Cybil War

1982 *The Animal, the Vegetable, and John D. Jones*
The Two-Thousand-Pound Goldfish

1983 *The Glory Girl*

1984 *The Computer Nut* (graphics by son Guy)
Gets her Pilot's license

1985 *Cracker Jackson*

1986 *The Not-Just-Anybody Family*
The Blossoms Meet the Vulture Lady
The Golly Sisters Go West

1987 *The Blossoms and the Green Phantom*
A Blossom Promise

1988 *Beans on the Roof*
The Burning Questions of Bingo Brown

1989 *Bingo Brown and the Language of Love*

1990 *Bingo Brown, Gypsy Lover*
Hooray for the Golly Sisters

1991 *Seven Treasure Hunts*
Wanted . . . Mud Blossom
The Moon and I

1992 *Bingo Brown's Guide to Romance*
Coast to Coast

1993 *McMummy*

1994 *The Dark Stairs: A Herculeah Jones Mystery*
The Golly Sisters Ride Again

1995 *Tarot Says Beware: A Herculeah Jones Mystery*

1996 *My Brother Ant*
Dead Letter: A Herculeah Jones Mystery
Tornado

1997 *Ant Plays Bear*
Death's Door: A Herculeah Jones Mystery

1998 *Disappearing Acts: A Herculeah Jones Mystery*

2000 *My Dog, My Hero*
Me Tarzan

THE MIDNIGHT FOX

A boy is stranded on a relative's farm for the summer and becomes fascinated by a black fox. When the fox starts attacking farm animals, it's up to Tom to try to stop his uncle from killing it.

THE SUMMER OF THE SWANS

Sara's mentally challenged brother becomes lost in the woods one night while looking for some swans they saw on a lake. While searching for her brother, Sara gains a new appreciation for the people in her life.

THE HOUSE OF WINGS

When ten-year-old Sammy is left with a grandfather he never met, the first thing he does is run away. While he waits for his parents to settle in the city and send for him, Sammy and his unusual grandfather form a bond while helping an injured sandhill crane.

THE 18TH EMERGENCY

Mouse lives his worst nightmare when he crosses the school bully and tries to put off being beaten up. While he awaits certain annihilation, Mouse comforts himself by remembering what to do in different emergencies like vampire attacks or quicksand.

AFTER THE GOAT MAN

Figgy has just made friends in his new neighborhood when his grandfather, known as the Goat Man, ends up on the nightly news. The grandfather has holed up in their old cabin with a shotgun, trying to prevent it from being torn down to make room for a highway.

THE PINBALLS

Carlie, Thomas J. and Harvey are three strangers who end up in the same foster home. Each begins to work through their own problems of neglect and abuse as they figure out how to live together.

THE NIGHT SWIMMERS

Retta's father leaves her in charge when he goes off to sing country music at night. Home alone, Retta forces her brothers to sneak swims in a stranger's pool after dark. When Johnny tries to be independent, he and Retta come to hate each other. Their mistrust and dislike soon lead to a near-tragedy.

THE TWO-THOUSAND-POUND GOLDFISH

Warren lives with his sister, his grandmother and his imagination. Hurt and confused about his parents who are on the run from the law, Warren makes up horror films to escape from his problems.

CRACKER JACKSON

Cracker is loyal to his old babysitter, Alma, who he fears is being beaten by her husband. Enlisting a friend to help, Cracker tries to get Alma out of a very complicated adult situation.

THE NOT-JUST-ANYBODY FAMILY

This is the first book in the Blossom family series. The book begins with Junior trying to fly with homemade wings. Maggie helps Vern break into jail to see Pap and helps break Junior out of the hospital and into the courthouse. This novel introduced the world to the wonderfully quirky Blossom clan.

THE GOLLY SISTERS GO WEST

This book began the Golly sisters series and follows Rose and May May as the zany sisters take their traveling song and dance act on the road in their covered wagon.

THE BURNING QUESTIONS OF BINGO BROWN

Bingo Brown falls in love as he tries to figure out his family, girls and life in general.

THE DARK STAIRS

Herculeah Jones was bound to be a sleuth with a private eye for a mother and a police detective for a father. She has a talent for finding dead bodies and for figuring out how they got that way. Herculeah is wonderfully fearless and determined and a total individual.

MAD MARY lives in the woods with vultures for watchdogs. Mary is a fascinating character who makes a tasty roadkill stew and has boxes of books lining her cozy cave. She rejected society after her wealthy father's home burned down around him, and while she's a definitely eccentric, the only thing "mad" about her is her name.

MOUSE likes to write labels in tiny letters on things like holes in his apartment building or on his sneakers. He also likes to feel prepared for whatever life may throw at him, like a vampire or gorilla attack or stepping into quicksand. He recites the steps to take in each kind of emergency to himself just to be sure he's ready.

MUD BLOSSOM is Betsy's favorite of her characters. Mud is Pap Blossom's dog and a truly faithful companion. When Pap is unhappy with him or something else has upset Mud, he retreats to his "misery hole" behind the front steps.

THE GOLLY SISTERS—Rose and May May—sing, dance, and purposely upstage each other. You never know what they'll do or say next, but you know you don't want to miss it.

BINGO BROWN is a fun, lovestruck sixth-grader trying to figure out girls and proud that he is mastering the fine art of what he calls "mixed–sex conversations."

HERCULEAH JONES is a teen who knows who she is and what she wants. She loves thrift store finds, solving mysteries and enlivening the otherwise dull existence of her loyal sidekick Meat.

1969 American Library Association Notable Book Award for *Trouble River*

1971 Newbery Medal for *The Summer of the Swans*

1977 American Book Award for *The Pinballs*

1977 Child Study Children's Book Award from the Bank Street College of Education

1979 Hans Christian Anderson Honors List for Promoting Concern for the Disadvantaged and Handicapped for *The Pinballs*

1980 Boston Globe Horn Book Award for *The Night Swimmers*

1981 National Book Award for *The Night Swimmers*
American Book Award for *The Night Swimmers*

1982 Parents Choice Award for literature for *The Animal, The Vegetable and John D. Jones*

1985 Parents Choice Award for literature for *Cracker Jackson*

1986 Parents Choice Award for literature for *The Not–Just–Anybody Family*

Betsy Byars has also received numerous state and other book awards over the years, including several Book of the Year selections from the Child Study Association of America.

Bach, Alice. "After the Goat Man." *New York Times Book Review* 15 Dec. 1974: 8.

Betsy Byars. Random House Publishers. Aug. 2001 <http://www.randomhouse.com/teachers/authors/byar.html>.

Byars, Betsy. *BetsyByars.com*. 07 Aug. 2001 <http://www.w3.iac.net/~feguy/betsybyars/index.html>.

Byars, Betsy. Home page. Indiana University. 07 Aug. 2001 <http://www.indiana.edu/~eric~eric_rec/ieo/bibs/byars.html

Byars, Betsy. "Ladders and Authority: Creating the Gift." *Journal of Youth Services in Libraries* 7.Wint (1994): 141-146.

Byars, Betsy. *The Moon and I*. Englewood Cliffs: Julian Messner, 1991.

Calloway-Schaefer, Judith. *The Alan Review*. Aug. 2001 <http://scholar.lib.vt.edu/ejournals/ALAN/fall97/schaefer.html>.

Contemporary Authors. Ed. Linda Metzger and Deborah A. Straub. Vol. 18. Detroit: Gale Research Company, 1986.

Cooper, Ilene. "Betsy Byars." *Booklist*. 15 Jan. 1993: 906-907.

Flagg, Fannie. "Bingo Brown and The Language of Love." *New York Times Book Review* 08 Oct. 1989: 34.

Kaye, Marilyn. "The Two-Thousand Pound Goldfish." *New York Times Book Review* 24 Nov. 1982: 24.

Kenney, Susan. "The Not-Just-Anybody Family." *New York Times Book Review* 15 June 1986: 38.

Newbery and Caldecott Medal Books: 1966-1975. Ed. Lee Kingman. N.p.: Horn Book, 1975.

Something About The Author Autobiography Series. Ed. Adele Sarkissian. Vol. 1. Detroit Michigan: Gale Research Company, 1986

Something About The Author. Ed. Kevin Hile. Vol. 80. Detroit: Gale Research Inc., 1995.

Something About The Author. Ed. Anne Commire. Vol. 46. Detroit: Gale Research Company, 1987.

Usrey, Malcolm. *Betsy Byars*. Vol. 636. New York: Twayne, 1995.

Note: *"Ladders and Authority" is a speech Byars gave that was printed in a book.*

www.iac.net/~feguy/betsybyars/
  [Betsy Byars' own site]
www.randomhouse.com/teachers/authors/byar.html
http://www.indiana.edu/~eric_rec/ieo/bibs/byars.html
http://scholar.lib.vt.edu/ejournals/ALAN/fall97/schaefer.html
www.betsyduffey.com
  [Byars' daughter Betsy's website. She has published 17 children's books]

RITA CAMMARANO is originally from Westchester, New York and currently lives in the Blue Ridge Mountains. She received her B.A. in History from Lynchburg College and her J.D. from the University of Richmond's T.C. Williams School of Law. She has had a historical piece published in *Cricket* (under the pen name Rita Giordano), and an essay broadcast on public radio. Ms. Cammarano is currently syndicating a column titled "The Other Side of Forty."

DATE DUE